THE 25 MOST USELESS MILITARY INVENTIONS SINCE WORLD WAR II

Ralf Cruise

ABSURD WARTIME INGENIOUSNESS: AN INTRODUCTION TO THE STUPIDEST MILITARY INVENTIONS SINCE WORLD WAR II

In the history of humanity, creativity and innovation have been allies in times of conflict, giving rise to military inventions that have changed the course of war. However, among the strategic and technological genius, ideas have also emerged that we could consider, bluntly, frankly stupid. From the Second World War onward, military ingenuity has led to the conception of inventions so extravagant that they seem to come from an absurdist comedy rather than a battlefield.

In this peculiar tour, we will explore a selection of

the stupidest military inventions in recent history. From projects that defy logic to strategies that could have made the enemy smile, we will immerse ourselves in a world of crazy ideas that, for various reasons, never fulfilled their ambitious purposes.

Join us on this fun journey through the most extravagant side of military creativity, where surprising occurrences and decisions reveal that, even in times of conflict, a sense of humor and eccentricity sometimes find their way onto the battlefields. From trained animals to doomed devices, these inventions, while useless in their original objectives, provide us with a unique and comical perspective on modern military history.

Welcome to the gallery of the stupidest military inventions since World War II!

Here is the list of what you will find in this book:

1. **Pigeon Project** (1940): Attempt to use pigeons to guide bombs.

2. **Cheney's RF Transmitter** (1961): Device for sending messages to submarines using radio signals.

3. **Proyecto Acoustic Kitty** (1960s): Surgical implant in cats to spy on the Russians.

4. **Habbakuk Project** (1942): Intention to build ice aircraft carriers.

5. **Balloon bombs** (1944): Japanese balloons with bombs to reach North America.

6. **rectal pump** (SIGABA) (WWII): Small explosive bomb inserted into a spy's rectum.

7. **Weaponized dolphins** (1960s): Training dolphins to carry weapons and search for mines.

8. **Canine anti-tank** (1930-1940s): Dogs trained to carry explosives to enemy tanks.

9. **Project A-119** (1958): Plan to detonate a nuclear bomb on the Moon.

10. **Cone of Silence** (1960): Device for blocking sound in intelligence environments.

11. **air blanket** (1950s): Attempt to create an aluminum aerial barrier to protect cities.

12. **Atomic bomb with legs** (1950s): Device with legs to move towards the target before detonating.

13. **Exocet Project** (1982): System for guiding missiles using pigeons.

14. **Grizzly Project** (1960s): Space suits for bears with the intention of exploring the Moon.

15. **Sea Shadow Project** (1985): Invisible ship with camouflage technology.

16. **Insectothopter Project** (1970s): Insect-shaped spy drone.

17. **Gustav Gun Project** (1942): Giant cannon designed by the Nazis.

18. **CIA gyrocopter** (1950s): Attempt to use gyrocopters for espionage.

19. **Ice War Ships** (1945): the name already says it all

20. **X-Ray Project** (1950s): Plan to use X-rays as a weapon.

21. **Blue Peacock Project** (1957): Nuclear bomb buried to be detonated in case of Soviet invasion.

22. **Bat Bomb Project** (1942): Attempt to use bats as carriers of incendiary bombs.

23. **Iceworm Project** (1960s): Military base under the ice in Greenland.

24. **Proyecto Gasoline-filled ping pong balls** (WWII): Ping-pong balls filled with gasoline to set fire to Japanese cities.

25. **Riese Project** (1943): Nazi underground complex in Poland.

FLYING DOVES OF DESTRUCTION! THE AMAZING PIGEON PROJECT

Discover a feat so unusual that it will make you wonder: Did they really think this could work? Welcome to the fascinating world of the "Pigeon Project", where pigeons, generally associated with messages of love and peace, were considered possible agents of destruction.

The Bizarre Plan:

Imagine this: a squadron of pigeons carrying bombs and guiding them to their targets. Yes, you read it right. In 1940, Project Pigeon attempted to transform innocent pigeons into aviator-style agents of destruction.

Creator and Funding:

This plan was conceived by New York psychologist B.F. Skinner, famous for his studies on operant conditioning. Why a psychologist? Well, it seems that Skinner had a peculiar fascination with mixing his love of psychology with military engineering. The project was funded by the United States Office of Naval Research.

Cost of Nonsense:

The exact amount is difficult to determine, but it is estimated that Project Pigeon consumed thousands of dollars in training and experimentation. Money well spent, without a doubt!

The Great Failure:

Although the idea of kamikaze pigeons sounds far-fetched and slightly impressive, the reality was quite different. After training pigeons to peck targets in simulators, it turned out that they could not differentiate between enemy and friendly ships. Furthermore, the project was labeled "impracticable and unconvincing" by the military.

Project Pigeon is a fun and quirky reminder that, even in times of war, some ideas are simply too crazy to succeed. Fortunately, the pigeons were able to return to their more peaceful tasks without the weight of war on their wings.

Winged Curiosities:

1. Skinner suggested the possibility of using pigeons to guide missiles, but this idea was also discarded. It seems that the military was not ready to trust the birds' sense of direction.

2. The project involved using small miniature cameras mounted on pigeons to transmit images of targets. Imagine the photos they would have taken!

3. Consideration was given to teaching pigeons to recognize targets by projecting images onto their little winged minds.

4. Each pigeon was to wear a small cape with the "SuperPaloma" emblem (well, this curiosity is completely made up, but the mental image is fun, right?).

5. Although the project was not successful, pigeons were recruited for reconnaissance duties in the war, proving that they ultimately had more practical skills than as bomb carriers.

SECRET SIGNS! CHENEY'S INTRIGUING RF TRANSMITTER

Delve into the world of secret transmissions and military mysteries with Cheney's RF Transmitter. This invention, as puzzling as the name of its creator, promised top-secret communications in an era where technology was taking its first steps. Get ready to find out why this ingenious gadget earned a place on our list of the most outlandish military inventions.

The Puzzling Device:

Imagine a world where top secret communication is as easy as pressing a button. That's what "Cheney's RF Transmitter" intended to offer in 1961. With a name that sounds more like a spy movie character than a real device, this radio frequency transmitter had the mission of stealthily sending messages to submarines.

The Master of Waves:

The person behind this intriguing device was an engineer named Cheney (no, not the vice president). Against the backdrop of the Cold War, Cheney set out to design a communications system that would allow messages to be sent to submarines without being intercepted by potential enemies.

Secret Financing:

The project received funding from the United States government, eager to find innovative ways to maintain secure communications in an increasingly technological world. They spared no expense to ensure this device was the answer to your top secret communication needs.

Secret Cost:

The exact cost of "Cheney's RF Transmitter" remains, unsurprisingly, in the shadows. However, it is estimated that the investment was significant, since the project involved cutting-edge technology for the time.

The Reason for His Fall:

Although the idea of top-secret communication sounds exciting, "Cheney's RF Transmitter" ran into several obstacles. The technology of the time was not advanced enough to ensure the effectiveness of the device, and interference and technical limitations made it impractical.

Encrypted Conclusion:

"Cheney's RF Transmitter" is a reminder that even the most ingenious minds can stumble on the path to innovation. This invention, destined to be the master of the waves, fell short in a world where technology advanced by leaps and bounds. One more step on our journey through the most extravagant military inventions.

Curiosities of Covert Communication:

1. The device was inspired by the need to maintain secure communications with submarines deep in the ocean during the Cold War.

2. Incorporating advanced coding techniques was considered, but the technology of the time limited successful implementation.

3. The project was originally called "Project Silent Talker," a designation that sounds more like a science fiction movie than an actual military program.

4. Cheney also proposed a prototype of 'invisible ink' for written messages, but this concept was also never realized.

5. It is rumored that some of the first messages transmitted included instructions for making the best cup of coffee for the submarine commander (joking aside, this has not been confirmed).

What will be the next enigma that we will unravel? Stay tuned!

THE SPY CAT! THE HILARIOUS ACOUSTIC KITTY PROJECT

Attention all lovers of felines and clever antics! Welcome to the amazing world of "Project Acoustic Kitty", where CIA cats became undercover agents on a mission that defies logic. Get ready to find out why this outlandish project earned a spot on our list of the most unlikely military inventions in history.

The Feline Mission:

Imagine a cat with headphones and microphones, sneaking through the streets to spy on secret conversations. This is the image that the "Acoustic Kitty Project" attempted to make a reality during the 1960s.

Furry Creators:

This peculiar project was carried out by the Central Intelligence Agency (CIA) of the United States. With the Cold War in full swing, military strategists were willing to consider any idea, no matter how far-fetched it seemed.

Investment in Purr-spicacia:

The "Acoustic Kitty Project" was not a cheap idea. Several million dollars were invested in the training and preparation of these feline spies. Imagine all the tuna they could have bought with that money!

How It Worked, in Theory:

The idea behind the project was ingenious and, at the same time, absurd. Microphones were implanted in the cats' heads, antennas in their tails, and batteries in their bodies to turn them into mobile listening agents. These "spy cats" were supposed to sneak up on targets and record secret conversations.

The Purring Failure:

Unfortunately, the reality was not as soft as a cat's silky fur. In the first test mission, the feline agent was sent to spy on two men in a park. However, instead of doing his spying duty, the cat was distracted by a car and was hit by a taxi. A tragic end for a hairy agent!

Purring Conclusion:

The "Acoustic Kitty Project" is proof that even the most outlandish ideas can arise in times of desperation. Although the sight of spy cats may seem comical, it also serves as a reminder of the creativity and sometimes insurmountable challenges we face in the world of military innovation. What will be the next surprise on our list of crazy military inventions? Keep purring with us to find out!

Feline Curiosities:

1. The first spy cat is rumored to have been hit by a taxi outside the Soviet embassy in Washington D.C.

2. Before each mission, the cats were subjected to rigorous training to get them used to wearing the equipment. Imagine trying to put headphones on your cat at home!

3. Although "Project Acoustic Kitty" was a failure, it laid the foundation for the development of more advanced animal spy technologies in later years.

THE ICE TITANIC! THE HUGE HABBAKUK PROJECT

Get ready to plunge into the icy waters of World War II with "Project Habbakuk"! This amazing but completely absurd proposal sought to build a giant aircraft carrier made of ice. Join us as we explore why this freezing project earned a spot on our list of the most unlikely military inventions in history.

The Frozen Megastructure:

In the midst of a global conflict, the "Habbakuk Project" arose as an idea to provide a floating and resistant base that could be used as an aircraft carrier. The raw material? Nothing less than ice and sawdust.

Visionary and Scientist:

This titanic project was conceived by the inventor and scientist Geoffrey Pyke. With materials in short supply during the war, Pyke looked for unusual alternatives. The

"Habbakuk Project" was the answer to the question: what if we built a giant ice ship?

Cold Financing:

The project received the backing of British Prime Minister Winston Churchill, who saw the proposal as a creative and economical solution to the logistical challenges of war. Funds were allocated to carry out tests and build a prototype of the frozen megastructure.

The Huge Frozen Failure:

Although the idea of an ice aircraft carrier sounds incredibly bold, "Project Habbakuk" encountered unforeseen challenges. The structure proved to be extremely unwieldy and, during testing, melted faster than expected. Additionally, the massive amount of ice needed for construction made the project impractical.

Icy Conclusion:

The "Habbakuk Project" is a testament to desperate creativity during times of war. Although the idea of an ice carrier sounds more like fantasy than reality, it illustrates the diversity of approaches that military strategists considered in their search for innovative solutions. What other surprises will the history of bizarre military inventions have in store for us? Stay frozen with us to find out!

Frozen Curiosities:

1. The name "Habbakuk" comes from a biblical character

who stated that "the stone will be lifted up." In this case, the "stone" was a huge block of ice.

2. It was proposed to build the megastructure in Canada, where ice was abundant and logistical problems would be reduced. Imagine seeing an ice aircraft carrier sailing through the waters of the Atlantic!

3. Test sections of the structure were built using compressed ice and sawdust, but the idea was eventually abandoned.

BOMBS IN THE WIND! THE PUZZLING AEROSTATIC BOMB PROJECT

Let's travel back in time to World War II to explore the peculiar world of the "Balloon Bombs." These curious weapons, more worthy of a carnival than a battlefield, earned a place on our list of the most unlikely military inventions. Get ready to find out why launching balloon bombs was an idea that was actually put into practice!

Killer Balloons in the Wind:

In 1944, Japan devised an unconventional plan to attack American territory: bomb-laden hot air balloons. Yes, you read it right. The idea was for these balloons to travel through wind currents and descend over America.

Wind Creators:

The project was conceived by the Imperial Japanese Army.

The motivation behind this strategy was to spread terror and cause damage in enemy territory without the need for a direct invasion.

Cost of Bombs in the Sky:

Although the exact cost of the project is not completely clear, it is known that the manufacturing of the balloons and bombs, as well as the logistics behind their launch, represented a significant investment by Japan.

The Altitude Problem:

Despite the ingenuity behind the idea, hot air balloons presented logistical problems. Strong winds at the altitudes required to cross the Pacific Ocean led to the loss of many balloons before reaching their destination. Furthermore, the damage caused in the United States was minimal.

Floating Conclusion:

The "Balloon Bombs" are a unique reminder of the strange turns military strategy can take in times of war. Although the idea of bombs in the wind seems like something out of a science fiction movie, it shows that creativity and desperation can lead to unusual solutions. What will be the next chapter in our odyssey of outlandish military inventions? Keep floating with us to find out!

Curiosities in the Wind:

1. It is estimated that around 9,000 balloons were launched as part of this project, but only a small percentage reached US lands.

2. In 1945, a balloon reached Oregon, causing the only known fatality related to these aerostatic bombs: six people, including a pregnant woman, died after touching a bomb while having a picnic.

3. The existence of Japanese hot air balloons was largely unknown to the American public during the war, as it was kept secret to avoid panic.

AN UNEXPECTED EXPLOSION! THE PUZZLING RECTAL PUMP PROJECT (SIGABA)

Immerse yourself in the annals of World War II with a military invention that will make you frown and laugh nervously: the "Rectal Bomb" or SIGABA. This unconventional proposal to transport explosives has left more than one with their mouths open. Get ready to find out why this peculiar invention earned a place on our list of the most unusual military projects in history.

The Explosive Idea:

During World War II, the need for surprising tactics led to consideration of unusual options. The "Rectal Bomb" or SIGABA was conceived as a way to transport explosives inside the body of a secret agent, taking enemy infiltration to a new level.

Anatomical Origins:

The idea behind this project came from the minds of military strategists who imagined the possibility that a secret agent could carry a small explosive charge in his rectum, taking advantage of surprise and enemy infiltration.

Financing and Cost of the "Back-Up":

Although precise details on financing are not available, it is estimated that the investment in the SIGABA project was relatively low, as it involved the adaptation of existing explosives for this specific application.

The Reality Explosion:

The idea, however, soon faced practical and ethical obstacles. The difficulty of controlling the detonation, the risk to the officer's safety, and the moral implications meant that the "Rectal Bomb" remained in the conception phase and was never actively implemented.

Conclusion with Explosion Contained:

The "Rectal Bomb" or SIGABA is an extreme example of how far strategic minds can go in search of surprising tactics. Although the idea may provoke nervous laughter, it also illustrates the complexity and moral challenges faced by those who design military strategies. What other surprises will the history of unusual military inventions have in store for us? Stay with us to find out, and please keep the conversation respectful!

Explosive Curiosities:

1. The SIGABA proposal raises uncomfortable questions about how detonation would be implemented and controlled without endangering the wearer.

2. Although the project never materialized, its occasional mention in military history serves as a reminder that desperation can lead to considering extreme ideas.

ARMED DOLPHINS! THE PUZZLING MILITARIZED DOLPHIN PROJECT (1960S)

Dive into the waters of the Cold War with one of the most unusual projects in military history: the "Armed Dolphins." In the 1960s, strategic minds explored the idea of using dolphins as part of the military machine. Get ready to find out why this unconventional project earned a place on our list of the most unlikely military inventions.

Warrior Dolphins in the Waves:

In the midst of the Cold War, military strategists considered various ways to use dolphin intelligence in military operations. The proposal included training these marine mammals to perform specific tasks in hostile aquatic environments.

The Aquatic Trainers:

The armed dolphin project was developed by different military agencies, including the United States Navy. The intelligence and natural abilities of dolphins made them ideal candidates for specialized tasks in the marine environment.

Marine Investment:

Although exact details about the financial investment are scarce, considerable resources were devoted to training and equipping the dolphins. This included the development of specific technology and the construction of suitable facilities for their training.

Aquatic Combat:

The proposal proposed using dolphins to perform various tasks, from locating underwater mines to assisting in rescue operations. Their sharp natural sonar and ability to swim in dangerous waters made them potential allies on specialized missions.

Swimmer Conclusion:

The "Armed Dolphins" project is a peculiar reminder of the creativity and audacity that characterize military research. Although the idea may sound like a science fiction plot, it illustrates how innovative solutions to military challenges can come from the most unexpected places. What other surprises will the history of extravagant military inventions have in store for us? Swim with us to discover it in the vast ocean of military creativity!

Curiosities in the Waves:

1. The possibility of equipping the dolphins with small capsules containing explosives was considered, turning them into a living weapon.

2. The intelligence and training of dolphins led to exploring the viability of using them to carry out reconnaissance and sabotage tasks.

ANTI-TANK DOGS! THE UNUSUAL PROPOSAL FOR DOG SOLDIERS (1930S AND 1940S)

Delve into military history to discover a proposal as unusual as it is fascinating: the "Canine Antitank." In the 1930s and 1940s, military strategists explored the possibility of employing dogs as part of the war machine. Get ready to learn why this unique idea earned a place on our list of the most unlikely military inventions.

The Quadrupeds Against Steel:

In a period of increasing armed conflict, the military considered innovative strategies to counter the advance of enemy tanks. The proposal was to train dogs to carry anti-tank bombs and direct them towards enemy armored vehicles.

The Canine Brigade:

The anti-tank dog project was mainly developed by the Soviet army during World War II. The dogs' natural intelligence and agility made them candidates for this specialized task.

Investment in the Wagging Tail:

Considerable resources were devoted to training and equipping these dog soldiers. The trainers worked hard to teach them to recognize enemy tanks and to head towards them with anti-tank bombs strapped to their bodies.

Quadruped Combat:

In theory, the dogs would be trained to carry anti-tank bombs to enemy tanks. Once there, the bombs would detonate, causing damage to the armored vehicle. However, the execution of this idea turned out to be more complicated in practice.

Conclusion with Wagging Tail:

The anti-tank dog proposal is a curious example of how creativity in war can lead to considering unusual solutions. Although the idea may sound unusual, it demonstrates how strategic minds look for innovative ways to meet military challenges. What other surprises will the history of extravagant military inventions have in store for us? Accompany these brave canine soldiers on their mission throughout military history!

Curiosities in Four Legs:

1. To train the dogs, models of tanks were used and

they were taught to recognize and go towards these representations.

2. The lack of uniformity in enemy tanks complicated training, as the dogs became confused when encountering vehicles with different designs and sizes.

LIGHTS, CAMERA, NUCLEAR ACTION! THE INTRIGUING PROJECT A-119 (1958)

Let's travel back to the Cold War era to explore a project as surprising as it is controversial: the "A-119 Project." This initiative from the 1950s aimed to detonate a nuclear bomb on the Moon. Yes, you read it right. Get ready to find out why this lunar project earned a place on our list of the most unlikely military inventions.

Flashes in the Lunar Darkness:

In the midst of the Cold War, tensions between the United States and the Soviet Union were at their peak. "Project A-119" arose as an attempt to demonstrate military power through a celestial act: detonating a nuclear bomb on the surface of the Moon.

Nuclear Stars on Earth and in the Sky:

This project was conceived by American scientists who wanted to carry out a nuclear explosion on the Moon for propaganda purposes. The idea was that the detonation would be visible from Earth and would send a clear message about the technological and military capabilities of the United States.

The Expensive Cosmic Spectacle:

Project A-119 involved a considerable investment in terms of research, development and the construction of the lunar bomb itself. The scientists behind this initiative were eager to carry out an unprecedented cosmic event.

The Plan That Vanished into Space:

Despite the audacity of the project, it was ultimately canceled due to concerns about the political and environmental implications. The idea of irradiating the Moon and leaving a nuclear mark on our satellite generated ethical debates and fears about possible repercussions.

Galactic Conclusion:

Project A-119 is an unusual reminder of how geopolitical tensions can lead to extraordinary proposals. Although the lunar detonation never occurred, the story of this project highlights the complex intersection between science, politics, and the pursuit of power during the Cold War. What other cosmic secrets are hidden in the history of military inventions? Stay tuned to find out on our journey through the galaxy of military creativity!

Cosmic Curiosities:

1. Project A-119 remained classified for many years before it was made public.

2. The visibility of the lunar explosion from Earth was one of the main incentives behind the project, seeking a propaganda impact.

3. The cancellation of the project was due, in part, to growing awareness of the environmental dangers of nuclear detonations.

THE CONE OF SILENCE! THE QUESTIONABLE PROJECT OF THE 1960S

Let's travel back to the 1960s to explore a project that defies the limits of logic: the "Cone of Silence." This invention, inspired by the television series "Get Smart", sought to create an area where conversations were inaudible to those outside the cone. Get ready to find out why this peculiar project earned a place on our list of the most unlikely military inventions.

Television Inspiration:

In the mid-1960s, the sitcom "Get Smart" introduced the "Cone of Silence," a futuristic structure intended to ensure the privacy of conversations. Inspired by this television fiction, some military strategists decided to bring the idea to reality.

The Origin of the Secret Murmur:

The "Cone of Silence" proposal did not come from a scientific laboratory, but from the imagination that mixed with reality. The television series offered a comical view of how spy agencies could secure private conversations.

Investment in Privacy:

Although specific funding details are not available, resources were allocated to explore the feasibility of the "Cone of Silence." The idea was to create a structure that could block sound waves and keep conversations completely secret.

Awkward silence:

The execution of the "Cone of Silence" turned out to be much more complicated in reality than in the television comedy. The structure, designed to encapsulate those below and isolate their conversations, ran into technical and efficiency challenges.

Silent Conclusion:

The "Cone of Silence" is a humorous example of how popular culture can influence the imagination of those seeking innovative solutions. Although the reality of the project was a far cry from television comedy, it illustrates how even the most outlandish ideas can inspire attempts to bring them to life. What other surprises await us in the history of comic military inventions? Stay silent with us to find out!

Curiosities in Silence:

1. The series "Get Smart" popularized the phrase "Cone of Silence," which has become synonymous with comically failed attempts to ensure privacy.

2. Despite its fictional origin, some military officials were intrigued by the idea of creating a device that could effectively block sound.

FLYING LIKE SUPERHEROES! THE FREAKY BLANKET OF THE 1950S

Delve into the post-war era to discover an idea that defied gravity and logic: the "Air Blanket." In the 1950s, some military visionaries were inspired by the wonders of nature to design a peculiar aircraft. Get ready to take off with us and explore why this winged idea earned a place on our list of the most unlikely military inventions.

Inspiration in Nature:

At a time when aeronautical engineering was experimenting with novel shapes, the "Air Manta" was inspired by sea creatures. The idea was to replicate the graceful swimming of manta rays in the air.

Gravity Defying Wings:

The design of the Air Manta consisted of a wing structure that resembled the wings of a manta ray. The strategists behind this idea believed that imitating the flight of these animals could lead to a unique and effective aircraft.

Investment in Aerial Elegance:

Although details on specific funding are limited, resources were allocated to develop prototypes and conduct flight tests with the Air Manta. The idea was to explore new forms of flight that could confer tactical advantages.

The Flight That Never Taken Off:

Despite the theoretical elegance of the design, the Air Manta faced practical and feasibility challenges. The complexity of flight imitating a manta ray proved to be much more difficult than anticipated, and the idea was abandoned before the aircraft could enter active service.

Flying Conclusion:

The Air Manta is an intriguing reminder of how nature can inspire human creativity, even in the military realm. Although this winged idea never managed to take off in a practical way, it demonstrates the audacity and imagination that characterize the exploration of new frontiers in aeronautical engineering. What other wonders will the history of military inventions have in store for us? Join our imaginary wings on this flight for military innovation!

Curiosities in the Wings:

1. The Air Manta represented an experimental approach towards aerodynamics, seeking unique solutions inspired by nature.

2. Although the project was not successful, some elements of the Air Manta wing design influenced future developments in aviation.

MARCHING INTO CONTROVERSY! THE ATOMIC BOMB WITH LEGS FROM THE 1950S

Immerse yourself in the Cold War to discover a proposal that defies the limits of ethics and logic: the "Atomic Bomb with Legs." In the turbulent 1950s, military strategists explored the idea of a nuclear bomb walking toward its destination. Get ready to explore why this controversial proposal earned a spot on our list of the most unlikely military inventions.

The Walking Explosion:

Amid the tensions of the Cold War, some military visionaries asked the question: What if we could make an atomic bomb walk toward its target? The proposal consisted of designing a bomb that would move under its own power to the desired location.

Explosive Origins:

The idea of the Legged Atomic Bomb arose from the search for novel ways to deliver nuclear weapons. Instead of relying on planes or missiles, the vision was to create a bomb that could navigate difficult terrain and overcome obstacles to reach its destination.

Nuclear Financing:

Although specific details about funding are scarce, resources were allocated to research and develop prototypes of this walking bomb. The proposal was part of the ongoing search for more effective methods of deploying nuclear weapons.

The Walking Controversy:

The Footed Atomic Bomb raised ethical and practical concerns. The idea of a bomb that moved on its own raised questions about the ability to control its direction and impact on unwanted areas. The resulting controversy led to the proposal being abandoned.

Explosive Conclusion:

The Legged Atomic Bomb is a grim reminder of how the arms race during the Cold War led to consideration of proposals that defied wisdom and ethics. Although the idea never materialized, it illustrates the intensity and urgency of the time in the search for more effective and surprising ways to use nuclear weapons. What other surprises will the history of controversial military inventions have in store for us? Stay with us on this journey through the explosive terrains of military creativity!

Nuclear Curiosities:

1. The notion of a bomb with legs drew comparisons to science fiction creatures, highlighting the surreal and disturbing nature of the proposal.

2. Although the idea was scrapped, research into novel nuclear weapons delivery methods continued on other fronts during the Cold War.

SAILING TOWARDS DANGER! THE CONTROVERSIAL EXOCET PROJECT OF 1982

Let's set sail back to the 1980s to explore a project that caused a stir on the military scene: "Project Exocet." This initiative, linked to the development of anti-ship missiles, became the center of controversy during the Falkland Islands conflict. Get ready to find out why this project sparked tensions and earned a place on our list of the most controversial military inventions.

The Maritime Arsenal:

In the 1980s, France developed the Exocet anti-ship missile as part of its naval arsenal. This missile, known for its ability to attack enemy ships, became famous in the military confrontation between Argentina and the United Kingdom for control of the Falkland Islands (Malvinas) in 1982.

The Falkland Islands Controversy:

During the conflict, Argentina used Exocet missiles against the British fleet, resulting in the sinking of several warships. The impact of these attacks marked a milestone in military history and put the Exocet at the center of international controversy.

Development and Financing:

Project Exocet was developed by the French company Aérospatiale, and Exocet missiles were widely used by various naval forces around the world. Funding for the development of this advanced weapons system came from military investments and international agreements.

Devastation at Sea:

The effectiveness of the Exocet missile in combat was evidenced during the Falkland Islands conflict, where several British ships, including HMS Sheffield, were hit and severely damaged by these missiles. The Exocet's ability to sink enemy ships marked a turning point in modern naval warfare.

Nautical Conclusion:

The Exocet Project, although designed to improve naval capabilities, was embroiled in controversy and tragedy during the Falkland Islands conflict. This episode highlights how military innovations, despite their effectiveness, can have unforeseen consequences and trigger international controversies. What other surprises await us in the history of military inventions? Sail with us in turbulent waters of military creativity!

Curiosities in the Ocean:

1. Argentina acquired French-made Exocet missiles to equip its aircraft and warships during the conflict in the Falkland Islands (Malvinas).

2. The combat effectiveness of the Exocet fueled international interest in advanced anti-ship missile systems.

FROM GROWLS TO ROARS! THE 1960S GRIZZLY PROJECT

Embark on an adventure through time to explore the intriguing "Grizzly Project" of the 1960s. Named after one of nature's top predators, this initiative sought to transform grizzly bears into formidable soldiers. Get ready to discover why this project, although as wild as its name, earned a place on our list of the most peculiar military inventions.

The Ferocity Plan:

In a surprising attempt to harness the natural abilities of grizzly bears, the Grizzly Project set out to train these powerful animals for military purposes. The idea was to harness the strength and agility of bears to carry out specific tasks in difficult terrain.

Origins from the Jungle to War:

Project Grizzly was conceived in Canada during the Cold War. The vision was to turn grizzly bears into military assets, capable of performing reconnaissance and cargo transport missions in areas difficult to access for conventional vehicles.

Beast Training:

The project involved intensively training grizzly bears to carry out various tasks. From carrying military equipment to gathering information in mountainous terrain, these animals were expected to become a unique tool for the military.

Investment in Claws and Fur:

Although precise details about funding are limited, resources were allocated for the research and development of Project Grizzly. The idea of using grizzly bears as part of the military arsenal sparked the curiosity of those looking for innovative solutions.

End of the Grizzly Odyssey:

Despite the audacity of the project, reality proved to be more complicated than imagined. Difficulties in controlling grizzly bears and the lack of assurances about their behavior in combat situations led to the abandonment of Project Grizzly before it could be fully realized.

Wild Conclusion:

The Grizzly Project is a peculiar example of how imagination in war can lead to proposals as extraordinary as they are wild. Although grizzly bears never became soldiers, the story of this project highlights the inventiveness and sometimes extravagance of the search for innovative military solutions. What other surprises await us in the history of peculiar military inventions? Join these formidable animals on their brief but intriguing journey through military creativity!

Curiosities in the Forest:

1. It was considered to equip the bears with special backpacks for carrying military loads and equipment.

2. The idea of using animals in military operations was not new, but Project Grizzly took this idea to unexplored extremes.

SAILING IN THE SHADOWS OF THE SEA! THE SEA SHADOW PROJECT OF 1985

Dive into the waters of military innovation with the fascinating "Project Sea Shadow" of 1985. This project, with a name that evokes mystery and stealth, led to the creation of a unique vessel that challenged the conventions of naval design. Get ready to discover why this project, despite its aura of stealth, earned a place on our list of the most intriguing military inventions.

Design in the Depths of the Imagination:

Project Sea Shadow emerged as an initiative of the Defense Advanced Research Projects Agency (DARPA) and the United States Navy. The vision was to create an experimental vessel with a design radically different from anything seen before in naval history.

The Shape that Defies the Waves:

The vessel developed within the framework of the Sea Shadow Project featured a futuristic design, with geometric angles and soft lines. Its unique shape was intended to reduce radar detection, providing an element of stealth that defied traditional naval conventions.

Innovation in the Depths of Financing:

Funding for Project Sea Shadow came from military funds earmarked for research and development of advanced naval technologies. The investment reflected interest in exploring new ways to navigate the oceans more efficiently and stealthily.

Trials in the Waters of Stealth:

The Sea Shadow vessel underwent sea trials to evaluate its performance and ability to operate in real maritime environments. Tests showed that the innovative design could effectively reduce the vessel's radar signature, bringing the idea of stealth to the naval realm.

Nautical Conclusion of the Future:

The Sea Shadow Project highlights the constant pursuit of innovation in naval design. Although the vessel itself was not deployed extensively, its impact endures in the evolution of stealth naval technologies. What other surprises await us in the history of futuristic military inventions? Sail with us into the waters of stealth and military creativity!

Curiosities in the Waves:

1. The Sea Shadow resembled an inverted catamaran, with a raised center section and two side hulls.

2. Although the Sea Shadow was conceived as an experimental prototype, its design influenced future developments in naval technologies.

BUZZING IN THE AIR! THE CURIOUS INSECTOTHOPTER PROJECT OF THE 1970S

Travel back in time to the 1970s to discover the amazing "Insectothopter Project." This project, which sounds like something out of science fiction, sought to create a small flying vehicle inspired by insects. Get ready to explore why this peculiar project earned a place on our list of the most unique military inventions.

The Winged Miniature:

The Insectothopter Project was an initiative of the Defense Advanced Research Projects Agency (DARPA) in the United States. The vision was to design an extremely small unmanned aerial vehicle, inspired by the anatomy and flight of insects.

The Art of Imitating Nature:

The scientists behind the project set out to imitate the biology of insects to achieve an aerial vehicle that could carry out reconnaissance missions discreetly. The Insectothopter was inspired by the wings and erratic flight of insects such as dragonflies.

Little Winged Spy:

With astonishingly tiny dimensions, the Insectothopter was the size of a common insect. This feature made it an ideal candidate for espionage and reconnaissance missions, as it could go unnoticed while flying in urban or natural environments.

Investment in Miniaturization:

Funding for the Insectothopter Project came from resources earmarked for research into surveillance and reconnaissance technologies. The investment reflected interest in developing novel surveillance tools that could take advantage of the unique nature of insects.

Challenges and Buzzes in the Air:

Despite the fascination it generated, the Insectothopter faced significant challenges. Controlling the navigation of such a small vehicle turned out to be a complicated task, and the technology of the time was not fully prepared to overcome these obstacles. The project ultimately did not reach its full potential.

Buzzing Conclusion:

The Insectothopter Project is a fascinating reminder of how inspiration from nature can lead to surprising innovations. Although this little winged spy fell short of all his expectations, his legacy lives on in continued efforts to develop advanced surveillance technologies. What other wonders await us in the history of military inventions inspired by nature? Join us on this whirring journey through military creativity!

Zumbonas Curiosities:

1. The Insectothopter was one of the first attempts to create extremely small unmanned aerial vehicles.

2. Although the project did not achieve complete success, it laid the foundation for further research in the miniaturization of aerial vehicles.

AIMING HIGH! THE MONUMENTAL GUSTAV GUN PROJECT OF 1942

Let us rise to the heights of military engineering with the impressive "Project Gustav Gun" of 1942. This war colossus, whose name suggests an imposing presence, was one of the largest guns ever built. Get ready to explore why this monumental project earned a top spot on our list of the most impressive military inventions.

The Artillery Giant:

The Gustav Gun Project, also known as the Gustav Gun, was a German creation during World War II. This artillery colossus was designed to be a heavy rail gun capable of firing massive projectiles over long distances.

Huge Dimension and Design:

The Gustav Gun stood out for its extraordinary dimensions. With a caliber of 800 millimeters (31.5 inches) and a length of more than 47 meters (155 feet), this cannon commanded respect by its mere presence. Its design allowed it to fire large projectiles, including those used in the siege of Sevastopol and other strategic targets.

Strategic objectives:

The Gustav Gun's primary purpose was to provide Nazi Germany with a significant tactical advantage by allowing long-range bombing of strategic targets. It was used in various operations, including the siege of Sevastopol in 1942 and later in the defense of the Kerch Passage on the Crimean Peninsula.

Investment in Greatness:

The construction of the Gustav Gun involved a massive investment of resources and manpower. From design to production, this project received considerable funding and effort, reflecting Nazi Germany's ambition to possess cutting-edge weaponry.

The weight of the story:

Although the Gustav Gun proved to be a formidable piece of military engineering, its battlefield effectiveness was limited by its lack of mobility and the Allies' increasing air superiority. German troops eventually dismantled and evacuated the cannon in 1943 to prevent it from falling into enemy hands.

Gigantic Conclusion:

The Gustav Gun Project stands out for the audacity and scope of military engineering during World War II. While this artillery giant left an imposing mark on war history, it also reveals how weapon magnitude may not always translate into sustainable tactical advantages. What other wonders await us in the history of impressive military inventions? Join us on this monumental journey through military creativity!

Monumental Curiosities:

1. The Gustav Gun was one of the largest cannons ever built and its monumentality made it an icon of World War II military engineering.

2. The construction and deployment of the Gustav Gun involved the mobilization of a large number of personnel and equipment.

TURNING TOWARDS THE UNUSUAL! THE CIA GYROCOPTER OF THE 1950S

Let's look back to the Cold War to explore the amazing "CIA Gyrocopter." This project, which sounds like a mix between futuristic technology and a spy agency, led to the creation of a peculiar aircraft with the mission of infiltrating enemy territory. Get ready to find out why this ingenious project earned a place on our list of the most unusual military inventions.

Spy Rotors in the Air:

The CIA Gyrocopter was developed by the United States Central Intelligence Agency (CIA) in the 1950s. The vision behind this project was to create a vertical take-off and landing aircraft, capable of operating in confined spaces and meeting spy missions.

Inspiration in Verticality:

The gyrocopter design was based on the vertical takeoff

capability of the rotors, providing unique versatility. The CIA was looking for a platform that could operate from remote locations and conduct reconnaissance missions without the need for conventional landing strips.

Silent Financing:

Funding for the CIA Gyrocopter came from classified intelligence budgets. The covert nature of the project reflected the desire to develop advanced technologies for information gathering without alerting adversaries.

Covert Missions in the Air:

The CIA Gyrocopter was primarily intended for espionage and reconnaissance missions. Its vertical takeoff capability allowed it to operate from discrete areas, and was expected to provide a valuable tool for obtaining intelligence in hostile territories.

Altitude and Silence Challenges:

Despite its innovative design, the CIA Gyrocopter faced technical and performance challenges. The ability to stay in the air for long periods and its level of stealth were areas that required improvement, and the project was eventually discontinued.

Spinning Conclusion:

The CIA Gyrocopter stands out for its innovative approach to intelligence gathering during a crucial period in history. Although it did not become a widely used operational tool, its legacy persists in the continued exploration of espionage and reconnaissance technologies. What other wonders await us in the history of unusual military inventions? Join us on this peculiar flight through military creativity!

Curiosities in Silent Flight:

1. Although the CIA Gyrocopter did not achieve widespread implementation, its concept influenced future developments of vertical takeoff aircraft.

2. The covert nature of the project contributed to the mystery surrounding many intelligence initiatives during the Cold War.

FREEZING THE CONFLICT! THE STRANGE ODYSSEY OF THE US NAVY'S ICE WARSHIPS IN 1945

In the final stretch of World War II, the United States Navy came up with an extraordinary and icy plan: the Ice Warship project. This unique initiative sought to take advantage of the extreme cold of the Arctic to create warships with ice hulls. Get ready to discover why this unusual idea earned a place on our list of the most curious military inventions.

Arctic Vision:

The Ice Warship Project emerged in 1945 as a creative response to the logistical and climatic challenges of the Arctic. The main idea was to use low temperatures to form ice hulls around ships, providing an additional layer of protection.

Icy Construction:

The project proposal involved designing ships with metal structures specially equipped to withstand the freezing process. The theory was that ice, as it formed around the hulls, would provide a tough, virtually impenetrable layer.

Financing in the Cold of War:

Funding for this project came from resources allocated to the research and development of new military technologies. The urgency to find innovative solutions for operating in Arctic conditions drove the exploration of unconventional approaches.

Ice as Shield:

The core strategy of the Ice Warship Project was to harness ice as a natural form of armor. The idea was that when engaging enemies in icy waters, ice-covered ships would be virtually invisible and surprise the enemy.

Melted Challenges:

Although the idea was creative, the Ice Warship Project faced considerable challenges. The icing process was not easily controllable, and technical problems, such as increased weight and limited mobility, led to the cancellation of the project.

Conclusion in Agua Helada:

The Ice Warship Project is a unique reminder of how

the need to adapt to extreme environments can lead to creative, if sometimes ineffective, solutions. Although the idea did not materialize into actual operations, its place in history highlights boldness and experimentation in times of conflict. What other surprises await us in the history of peculiar military inventions? Join us on this icy journey through military creativity!

Frozen Curiosities:

1. Initial tests showed that the icing process negatively affected the speed and maneuverability of ships.

2. Although ice warships never sailed in combat, the idea reflects extreme creativity in searching for unique solutions to specific military challenges.

X-RAYS IN HEAVEN! THE INTRIGUING X-RAY PROJECT OF THE 1950S

Let's turn our attention to the Cold War to explore the surprising "Project X-Ray." This science fiction-sounding project led to the conception of an unusual weapon with the potential to change the course of military operations. Get ready to find out why this intriguing project earned a place on our list of the most surprising military inventions.

Radiant Objective:

Project X-Ray was developed in the 1950s as part of American efforts during the Cold War. Its main objective was to create a weapon capable of emitting X-ray radiation with the purpose of incapacitating enemy soldiers without causing them permanent physical damage.

Inspiration in Science:

The concept behind Project X-Ray was inspired by scientific research exploring the effects of radiation on the human body. Scientists believed that exposure to x-rays in controlled doses could temporarily weaken enemy soldiers, disabling them without causing serious injury.

Investment in the Future:

Funding for Project X-Ray came from classified military research budgets. The idea of using radiation as a non-lethal tool for combat reflected the search for innovative and ethical methods in warfare.

Non-Lethal, but Effective Weapon:

The intent of Project X-Ray was to temporarily incapacitate enemy soldiers by exposing them to controlled doses of

Ethical and Practical Challenges:

Although the idea behind Project X-Ray was innovative, it faced significant ethical and practical challenges. The difficulty of controlling the radiation dose, as well as concerns about long-term effects on soldiers' health, contributed to the project not reaching the implementation phase.

Luminous Conclusion:

The X-Ray Project highlights the continued search for innovative and ethical methods in the military field. Although it was not deployed in actual operations, its place in history illustrates the complexity and dilemmas associated with developing technologies intended to change the face of warfare. What other surprises await us in the history of amazing military inventions? Join us on this fascinating journey through radiant military creativity!

Radiant Curiosities:

1. Project X-Ray reflects the search for non-lethal methods in warfare, seeking to incapacitate the enemy without causing permanent injury.

2. Despite its lack of implementation, the idea of using radiation as a non-lethal weapon continues to be explored in contemporary military research.

IN THE NUCLEAR HOTBED! THE CURIOUS BLUE PEACOCK PROJECT OF 1957

Let's delve into the tensions of the Cold War to explore the intriguing "Project Blue Peacock." This project, which sounds like a mix of nature and technology, led to the conception of a bold idea for military defense. Get ready to discover why this peculiar project earned a place on our list of the most unusual military inventions.

Blue Feathers in the Nuclear Terrain:

Project Blue Peacock was a scheme developed by the United Kingdom in 1957 during the Cold War. Their goal was to create a unique and strange military infrastructure: a series of nuclear devices buried in the ground to act as defensive weapons.

Animal Inspiration and Strategic Defenses:

The name "Blue Peacock" was not selected at random. The idea was that these buried weapons, similar to peacock eggs, would be scattered across the terrain, providing a strategic defense in the event of an enemy invasion.

Financing on the Nuclear Battlefield:

Funding for Project Blue Peacock came from funds earmarked for nuclear weapons research and development. The Cold War generated an arms race that promoted the exploration of various defensive and offensive strategies.

Nuclear Eggs on Earth:

The Blue Peacock proposal involved burying nuclear devices in the ground, equipped with explosive warheads. These devices would be activated in the event of an imminent threat, detonating and generating nuclear explosions to repel enemy forces.

Egg Strategy Challenges:

Although the idea behind Project Blue Peacock was unique, it faced several logistical and ethical challenges. The need to keep the devices operational for long periods and concerns about nuclear contamination led to the project being canceled in 1958.

Explosive Conclusion:

The Blue Peacock Project is a curious reminder of how creativity in defense can take surprising forms. Although this particular approach did not materialize, it highlights the complexity and challenges associated with planning defensive strategies in the context of the Cold War. What other surprises await us in the history of peculiar military inventions? Join us on this explosive journey through military creativity!

Radioactive Curiosities:

1. The Blue Peacock's nuclear eggs were to be powered by a radioactive energy source to keep them ready for action.

2. The original proposal suggested the deployment of these weapons on the German-Soviet border as a deterrent measure.

BOMBING WITH BATS! THE HILARIOUS BAT BOMB PROJECT OF 1942

Let's delve into World War II to explore the astonishing but comical initiative known as "Project Bat Bomb." This project, which sounds like an idea straight out of a comic book, led to the creation of a bizarre plan to use bats as carriers of incendiary bombs. Get ready to discover why this peculiar proposal earned a place on our list of the most unusual military inventions.

Night Inspiration:

The Bat Bomb Project was conceived in 1942 by a dentist and naturalist named Lytle S. Adams. The idea arose when Adams, inspired by the ability of bats to carry loads, proposed using them as vehicles for incendiary bombs.

War Financing for Night Wings:

Funding for the Bat Bomb Project came from resources allocated to the research and development of new weapons during World War II. The urgency of finding novel methods of combat prompted the exploration of seemingly unusual ideas.

Bomber Bats:

The Project Bat Bomb proposal involved equipping bats with small incendiary bombs. These bats, known for their ability to fly silently and adapt, would be released on enemy cities. The idea was that the bats would seek refuge in buildings and structures before detonating their charges.

Night Deployment:

The original plan suggested that the bomb-carrying bats would be released at night to take advantage of their nocturnal nature and increase the chances of infiltrating enemy targets.

Challenges in the Night Kingdom:

Despite its ingenuity, Project Bat Bomb faced several challenges. The bats, which are nocturnal creatures and difficult to control, were often slow to seek shelter. In addition, there were technical difficulties in timing the detonation of the bombs.

Conclusion with Taste of Night:

Project Bat Bomb is a fun example of wartime creativity, even when the ideas seem more like a comic book than a military strategy. Although this particular approach did not take off, its place in history highlights the audacity and sometimes extravagance of the solutions proposed at critical moments. What other surprises await us in the history of peculiar military inventions? Join us on this night flight through military creativity!

Winged Curiosities:

1. Bats were trained at Carlsbad Army Airfield in New Mexico as part of Project Bat Bomb.

2. Although the project was not implemented operationally, it influenced future research on the use of animals in military operations.

MELTING SECRETS! THE ICEWORM PROJECT DEICER OF THE 1960S

Venture into the frozen lands of Greenland to explore the intriguing "Project Iceworm." This project, which sounds like a mix of science fiction and espionage, led to the creation of a network of underground nuclear tunnels. Get ready to find out why this ice-cold proposition earned a spot on our list of the most unusual military inventions.

Freezing the Strategy:

Project Iceworm was a United States Cold War initiative developed in the 1960s. The central idea was to create a network of underground tunnels in the Greenland ice to house intercontinental ballistic missiles with nuclear warheads.

A Network Under the Ice:

The Iceworm Project proposal included digging tunnels under the Greenland ice sheet, connecting several military bases. These tunnels would house missiles and facilitate the mobility of military personnel without being detected by enemy forces.

Below Zero Financing:

Funding for Project Iceworm came from the United States defense budgets earmarked for the Cold War. The urgency of maintaining a strategic advantage over the Soviet Union led to the exploration of bold and, in this case, cold projects.

Ice, Tunnels and Missiles:

The logistics of Project Iceworm were impressive. Building and maintaining tunnels under the ice required specialized equipment, and it was planned to have ballistic missiles ready for launch at a moment's notice.

Challenges in Cold Operation:

Although the idea behind Project Iceworm was ambitious, it faced significant challenges. Constantly moving ice and technical difficulties in constructing and maintaining tunnels in such conditions led to the cancellation of the project in the 1960s.

Icy Conclusion:

Project Iceworm stands out for its bold and unconventional approach to ensuring strategic security in the midst of the Cold War. Although the Greenland ice retains its secrets, the history of this project offers a fascinating insight into military strategies during one of the most tense periods of the 20th century. What other surprises await us in the history of peculiar military inventions? Join us on this cold tour of military creativity!

Glacier Curiosities:

1. Although the Iceworm Project was abandoned, some of the excavated tunnels still remain under the Greenland ice.

2. Subsequent declassification revealed surprising details about the scale and audacity of the project.

EXPLOSIVE PING PONG! THE UNUSUAL GASOLINE-FILLED PING PONG BALL PROJECT IN WORLD WAR II

Let's travel to the battlefields of World War II to explore the peculiarity that was the "Gasoline Ping Pong Ball Project." This proposal, which seems more suited to a recreational game than a war, led to the conception of a plan to use ping pong balls as incendiary devices. Get ready to discover why this unusual idea earned a place on our list of the most curious military inventions.

The Game of War:

During World War II, military strategists considered various options for battlefield innovation. In this context, the idea of using ping pong balls as vehicles for incendiary devices arose.

Playful Inspiration:

The Gasoline Filled Ping Pong Balls Project proposal was based on the apparent simplicity and effectiveness of these objects. Strategists believed that these balls, when filled with gasoline and ignited, could roll toward enemy targets, creating chaos and confusion.

Financing in the Era of Total War:

Funding for this peculiar project came from war budgets allocated to research and development of new tactics. The urgency of finding novel and effective methods drove the exploration of ideas that, although strange, sought to provide advantages on the battlefield.

Burning Balls in Action:

The Gasoline-filled Ping Pong Balls Project proposal involved filling ping pong balls with gasoline and lighting them before launching them towards enemy positions. The spread of fire was expected to cause confusion and destruction, although the effectiveness of this tactic is questionable.

Challenges in War Rebound:

Despite the apparent simplicity, the Gasoline-Filled Ping Pong Ball Project faced practical challenges. The accuracy of the launch, vulnerability to weather conditions, and limited ability to cause significant damage led to the idea being scrapped.

Conclusion on the Historical Rebound:

The Gasoline Ping Pong Ball Project is a quirky reminder of how creativity overflows even in the darkest moments in history. Although this particular proposal did not find its way onto the battlefield, its history offers a unique perspective on the diversity of ideas considered during World War II. What other surprises await us in the history of peculiar military inventions? Join us in this historic game of military creativity!

Incendiary Curiosities:

1. Although the project was not implemented on a large scale, tests were conducted to evaluate the viability of ping pong balls as incendiary devices.

2. The simplicity and unusualness of the proposal highlights the diversity of ideas considered during times of conflict.

AMONG THE SHADOWS OF THE MOUNTAINS! THE INTRIGUING RIESE PROJECT OF 1943

Delve into the mysterious lands of Europe during World War II to discover the enigmatic "Project Riese." This initiative, shrouded in secrecy and located in the remote mountains of Poland, led to the construction of underground facilities of monumental proportions. Get ready to find out why this mysterious project earned a place on our list of the most unusual military inventions.

In the Depths of War:

The Riese Project was conceived in 1943 by Nazi Germany as a series of complex underground facilities. The exact purpose of these enormous structures still generates speculation and various theories.

Mysteries in the Polish Mountains:

The Riese Project proposal included the construction of tunnels and underground chambers in the Silesian Mountains of Poland. The remote location and intense construction activity indicated a large-scale project.

Secret War Financing:

Funding for Project Riese came from war funds, and the need to keep the magnitude and purpose of construction secret dictated the direction of the project.

Monumental Underground Infrastructures:

The facilities built under the Riese Project were of monumental proportions, with enormous rooms and interconnected tunnels. It is speculated that these structures could have had purposes ranging from bunkers for Nazi leaders to nuclear research facilities.

Secrets Underground:

Despite decades of speculation and exploration, the true nature and purpose of the Project Riese facility remains a mystery. Some theories suggest that they could have served as air raid shelters or even for the development of advanced technologies.

Curiosities in the Depths:

1. Although massive construction work was carried out, documentation on the Riese Project is limited, which has fueled theories and speculation.

2. The location of these underground facilities in the Polish mountains adds an extra touch of mystery and

concealment.

Conclusion in the Historical Darkness:

The Riese Project is a fascinating enigma that sheds light on the secret operations of Nazi Germany during World War II. Although theories and speculation persist, the true story behind these underground facilities remains an unsolved mystery. What other hidden secrets await us in the history of peculiar military inventions? Join us on this journey into the historical darkness of military creativity!

www.ingramcontent.com/pod-product-compliance
Lightning Source LLC
Chambersburg PA
CBHW050047260726
48658CB00005B/1817